The Official

Celtic Football Club
Annual 2006

Written by Douglas Russell

A Grange Publication

© 2005. Published by Grange Communications Ltd., Edinburgh, under licence from Celtic Football Club. Printed in the EU.

ISBN 1 902704 96 7

£6.99

Contents

Gordon Strachan –
The Man In Charge

In the early summer of 2005, Gordon Strachan, both a student of the game and a renowned coach, was confirmed as the new manager of Celtic following the emotional departure of Martin O'Neill. Indeed, the Edinburgh-born 48-year-old is the same age as his predecessor was when the Irishman himself arrived at the club in June 2000. Strachan had previously managed Coventry and Southampton in the English Premiership and, earlier than that, enjoyed huge success as a player in both Scotland and England.

After moving from Dundee to Aberdeen, the midfielder's football career really took off when Alex Ferguson was appointed manager of the Pittodrie outfit and Strachan was an important member of the granite city team that went on to win two Scottish League titles, three Scottish Cups, the 1983 European Cup Winners' Cup and the European Super Cup. Then, swapping one shade of red for another in 1984, Manchester United manager Ron Atkinson persuaded him to join the Red Devils. Two years later, he was reunited with Ferguson when the Scot accepted the position of manager at Old Trafford. At the time, Liverpool were the strongest of the strong in England and Strachan's five year term with United yielded only one real success – the FA Cup triumph of 1985. That silverware season, he also scored 19 goals.

Joining Howard Wilkinson's Leeds United in 1989, the wee man was, in a sense, re-born and helped the Midlands side to the old Second Division title in his first season with them. Back in the top flight, even greater success followed and, for 35-year-old captain Strachan, it was the 1992 Championship along with Footballer of the Year accolade in England at the same time. He had become the only player to win this prestigious award on both sides of the border. In the blue of Scotland, he won 50 caps and played in both the 1982 and 1986 World Cups. Few fans will ever forget his

stunning goal against West Germany in the 1986 Mexico tournament and his subsequent 'leg-over advertising hoarding' celebrations!

After a spell as assistant to Ron Atkinson at Coventry, he duly became manager of the Sky Blues and, in Season 1996/97, guided them to 11th spot in the Premiership equalling their best-ever final position in this league. South coast Southampton was the next port of call and another 11th position before taking Saints to the FA Cup final (and top half of the championship table with 8th place) in the 2002/03 period. Although Arsenal won the final 1-0, Southampton had qualified for the UEFA Cup competition, their first European venture since back in 1984/85. Interestingly, both Coventry and Southampton were second-bottom at the time of Strachan's appointment. He eventually left Southampton in February 2004.

At Celtic Park, he is following in the footsteps of several truly great men including Willie Maley, Jimmy McGrory, Jock Stein, Billy McNeill and, of course, Martin O'Neill. Time will tell if the wee man achieves the level of success associated with those legends.

Last season, Celtic won more league games than any other SPL side. Match by match, here is a reminder of all 30 victories and the 77 goals scored in those winning championship clashes.

August 2004
8.8.04: Celtic 2 Motherwell 0
The champions began the defence of their SPL title when Motherwell provided the opening day's opposition. Celtic took the lead very early in the first half when then team captain (and 2003/04 Player of the Year) Jackie McNamara lashed a powerful shot past keeper Marshall from the edge of the box following a lay-off by McGeady. Ten minutes into the second period, it was all over as a contest when Sutton, from close range, buried a low Alan Thompson cross to double the score.

14.8.04: Kilmarnock 2 Celtic 4
At Rugby Park the following Saturday, Kilmarnock (who had won their own opening encounter at Easter Road) certainly made a game of it and, indeed, took the lead twice in the first forty-five before John Hartson (a close range shot) and Alan Thompson (a delightful left foot finish after rounding the keeper) claimed first and second equaliser respectively. With the game evenly balanced at 2-2, defender Lilley was then dismissed for deliberate handball (when Chris Sutton had a clear scoring chance) before Thompson gave Celts the lead with the resultant free-kick. The second period was relatively straightforward and it came as no real surprise when the visitors extended their lead with a Hartson header from Thompson's free-kick in seventy minutes.

22.8.04: Inverness CT 1 Celtic 3
For their second Sunday league game in three weeks, Celtic travelled north to Aberdeen where, initially, newly promoted Caley Thistle played their home fixtures. Balde was back in the heart of the defence but Chris Sutton was missing through injury, with Henri Camara taking his place in attack. After the Spaniard Juanjo had been dismissed early in the first half following a clash with Neil Lennon, Celts took the lead with a fine John Hartson header before Barry Wilson's subsequent penalty equaliser. Despite missing a spot-kick in the second period, Stilian Petrov made amends with a superb dipping volley to restore his side's advantage. Welsh wizard Hartson (with his fourth league goal in two games) then made it three from close range after keeper Brown failed to hold a Valgaeren effort.

29.8.04: Celtic 1 Rangers 0
With Chris Sutton still injured, John Hartson and Henri Camara led the line in the first Old Firm clash of the campaign. New signing Juninho (sporting the No7 jersey) was on from the start and, indeed, ended the game with a richly deserved man of the match award. In truth, the Ibrox side defended well and the game seemed to be heading for a no-score draw. However, just like the final Old Firm clash of last season, there was a deadly sting in Celtic's tail just before the final whistle. On this occasion, Alan Thompson hit a tremendous left-foot drive which swerved before going in off the bar with Klos beaten from distance. As well as being five points ahead of Rangers in the SPL race, Celtic had now created a record of seven successive Old Firm wins.

September 2004
11.9.04: Celtic 3 Dundee 0
Henri Camara claimed a double - his first Celtic goals - with one in either half of a relatively straight forward home win. John Hartson was also on the score sheet for the defending champions with his fifth in as many league games since the start of the season.

19.9.04: Hibernian 2 Celtic 2
Ex-Celt Tony Mowbray's young Hibernian side led twice at Easter Road but strikes from Camara (a blistering finish) and then Hartson ensured that Celtic were back on level terms prior to the interval. Although O'Neill's men created the better of the chances during the second period, the game ended all square and, despite this loss of two points, Celtic remained four clear at the top of the table.

25.9.04: Celtic 3 Dunfermline 0

Taking his tally to five goals in three SPL matches, Henri Camara performed impressively again and netted another brace (one in each forty five) against the new look red and black of Dunfermline. The opener, however, came from defender Stan Varga, following an Alan Thompson corner after some twenty minutes of play. The Celts had now hit eighteen goals in the opening seven games of the 2004/05 campaign.

October 2004
3.10.04: Dundee United 0 Celtic 3

Having lost four goals at Motherwell and five at Kilmarnock in previous games, Dundee United were three behind at the interval as the Bhoys put on their Sunday best to completely outclass Ian McCall's team. In nine minutes, Chris Sutton (his first league start since the opening day of the season) headed home from a Petrov corner before the Bulgarian himself finished well from a tight angle to make it two. Then, after Camera had been fouled in the box, Sutton stepped forward to beat Jarvis from the penalty spot.

16.10.04: Celtic 3 Hearts 0

Two weeks later, with centre-backs Balde and Valgaeren both missing through injury, two goal hero Chris Sutton was in central defence with Hartson and Camara up front. Indeed it was the star from Senegal who broke the deadlock just prior to the interval with a thumping left foot volley. Some twelve minutes after the break, the pivotal second goal was scored by Juninho – his first for the club since arriving from Middlesbrough – after a penetrating run and exchange of passes with John Hartson. Then, after Hearts captain Pressley had missed from the spot, a Hartson header near the end (his seventh league goal so far) completed the day's entertainment.

24.10.04: Livingston 2 Celtic 4

This Almondvale victory meant that Celtic's unbeaten SPL away record now stretched beyond eighteen months. In a game of nine bookings, Stilian Petrov gave Celtic the lead before many fans had even taken their seats with Henri Camara then making it two inside the quarter of an hour mark on a rather waterlogged pitch. John Hartson and Chris Sutton (from the tightest angle) brought the team's tally to four before O'Brien pulled one back on the stroke of half time. The same player netted again to narrow the gap early in the second period but, in truth, Celtic ran out comfortable winners.

27.10.04: Celtic 2 Aberdeen 3
A quite astonishing league clash at Celtic Park ended with all three points heading north. Almost unbelievably, visitors Aberdeen had gone two ahead after only six minutes of play before John Hartson reduced the deficit just before the break. It was the Welshman again to the rescue with his tenth goal in all competitions when he made it 2-2 in the second half but the real drama was still to come, with substitute Stewart netting the winner in added time.

30.10.04: Motherwell 2 Celtic 3
The month ended with a game which was finely balanced at 2-2 until deep into the second period, before Celtic delivered the fatal blow. In truth, the visitors had been well in control and leading 2-0 with twenty five minutes to go, courtesy of goals from McGeady and Thompson, before Motherwell netted twice in just four minutes for what might have been one of the comebacks of the season. Then, with thirteen minutes left, Craig Beattie hit a beauty from McNamara's pass to ensure that it really was all over for Terry Butcher's Fir Park men.

November 2004
6.11.04: Celtic 2 Kilmarnock 1
McGeady was to the fore again the following week when the youngster claimed the opener at Celtic Park with a glorious free-kick over the defensive wall just before the half time break. In the second period, Alan Thompson slotted home from the penalty spot after a foul on Camara, before Nish claimed a consolation in the closing minutes. Interestingly, in all competitions, this had been Celtic's seventh game in just twenty one days.

13.11.04: Celtic 3 Inverness CT 0
Deployed in midfield, Chris Sutton marked his return from injury with a goal in three minutes when he netted from McGeady's accurate cross into the box. Surprisingly, there was no additional scoring in the first half but John Hartson's double in the second period (a volley from the edge of the 6-yard box and a header from close range following good play by Jackie McNamara on both occasions) took the big man's tally to twelve in the SPL.

20.11.04: Rangers 2 Celtic 0
In a heated clash, Celtic failed to score against Rangers for the first time since Martin O'Neill had taken charge of the club. First half goals from Novo and Prso did all the damage before Alan Thompson was red-carded after a clash with Lovenkrands. Chris Sutton's dismissal after the break ensured that it was a day to forget although, despite this defeat, Celtic still remained at the top of the table - albeit by just one point.

28.11.04: Dundee 2 Celtic 2
The Old Firm roles in that one point scenario situation were reversed the following week when Rangers won at home and Celtic drew at Dens Park against a Dundee side already facing the prospect of relegation. After English striker Lovell had given Jim Duffy's outfit a lead on the half hour mark, Henri Camara equalised from close range early in the second period. John Hartson then made it two, also from close-in, following a mazy McGeady run past several defenders in dark blue but it was that man Lovell again who grabbed the headlines with a chip past Hedman from the tightest of angles for a share of the spoils.

December 2004
4.12.04: Celtic 2 Hibernian 1
It was back to winning ways in December with John Hartson netting in each half of the all-green clash with Hibernian. In addition to his brace of goals, he was a class apart and tormented the visiting rearguard in a memorable man of the match display. The home fans roared to acclaim his flashing penalty box header from McGeady's corner just after the 15-minute mark and were singing his praises yet again near the end when he finished a move once again involving the youngster. This cancelled out Hibernian's entirely merited equaliser by defender Caldwell, some minutes earlier.

12.12.04: Dunfermline 0 Celtic 2
Although Chris Sutton opened the scoring early-on with a header from inside the six yard box, it was the second goal of the game that really had the fans on their feet when Stilian Petrov (sporting black tights, possibly to combat any plastic pitch burns) hit a spectacular scissor-kick volley which screamed past the helpless Stillie. It was the Bulgarian's first goal in eleven matches. Dunfermline rarely threatened in a game where the official attendance was only 7650.

18.12.04: Celtic 1 Dundee United 0

Although there was just one goal separating the teams at the final whistle, this was more like a stroll in the park than a close encounter! It really was the most convincing victory despite the fact that Chris Sutton's simple near post header was the only time that the ball actually crossed the line as United keeper Bullock had defied Celtic time after time with a series of superb stops.

26.12.04: Hearts 0 Celtic 2

This Boxing Day clash in the capital was a meaty affair with the visitors scoring both before and after the break courtesy of McGeady and Petrov respectively. The Celtic fans had not forgotten that Tynecastle was the venue for the teenager's first team debut last season and his early left foot strike was greeted with as much relish as his opener back then. In the second half, Petrov made certain with another one of his trademark power strikes - after Chris Sutton had created the chance for him – and the holiday celebrations continued in at least one part of the ground.

January 2005

2.1.05: Celtic 2 Livingston 1

Relegation threatened Livingston fought back well after going behind to a John Hartson header with some sixteen minutes on the clock. Indeed, the Lions equalised through Hamilton to make it 1-1 at the break. A disputed penalty converted by Chris Sutton, however, was enough to ensure an advantage of three points at the top of the table after rivals Rangers dropped two at Tannadice the same day.

16.1.05: Aberdeen 0 Celtic 1

With the manager having to select from only sixteen players at Pittodrie on a bitter day in the north-east, Celtic proved once again that, despite being bruised and battered, their will to win was as strong as ever. Chris Sutton's first half deflected goal was the difference between the sides in a game that began with both Jackie McNamara and Bobo Balde in the starting line-up, despite neither player being fully fit.

22.1.05: Celtic 2 Motherwell 0

Both the crowd and keeper Rab Douglas had difficulty keeping warm during this one-sided SPL affair. Chris Sutton was involved in both goals, laying on the first for Stilian Petrov before hitting the second himself after

Alan Thompson's through ball pierced the claret and amber rearguard. After the game, Motherwell manager Terry Butcher suggested that both Celtic and Rangers had outgrown Scottish Football.

30.1.05: Kilmarnock 0 Celtic 1

The month ended with another important victory. The remarkable Chris Sutton (many would suggest Martin O'Neill's best-ever buy) claimed his seventh goal in just eight games and another three vital championship points were tucked away. The decisive strike, in the latter stages of the first half, was from the penalty spot after Invincible was adjudged to have handled in the area.

February 2005

20.2.05: Celtic 0 Rangers 2

Celtic played only one SPL game in the month of February - the third Old Firm clash of the campaign. Prior to this game, Celtic had won nine of the previous eleven home clashes with Rangers. Indeed, the Ibrox side's last victory at Celtic Park was way back in March 2000, some five years earlier. Despite completely dominating the first period, it was still 0-0 at the interval thanks to a series of great saves by Waterreus. Rangers, it must be said, were the better side in the second period although their opener came as a result of an error when Rab Douglas failed to hold a Vignal effort. Striker Novo claimed the visitors' second goal.

March 2005

2.3.05: Celtic 3 Dundee 0

With Celtic legend Billy McNeill in attendance for this Wednesday night fixture (he was celebrating birthday number 65), the home crowd had to wait five minutes into the second period before their own celebrations could begin. Stilian Petrov eventually broke the deadlock with a diving header from McNamara's cross. Not to be outdone, Bobo Balde also headed home but the big man's tally was double that of the Bulgarian with two goals in the last ten minutes of the game.

6.3.05: Hibernian 1 Celtic 3

Much was expected from Hibernian at Easter Road four days later but the stiff challenge never really materialised and Celtic dismissed Tony Mowbray's young side with relative ease. First half goals from Petrov and Hartson – a Bulgarian right foot drive and Welsh half-volley – did all the damage before Craig Bellamy's super solo effort in the second

period (his first SPL goal) inflicted further pain on the home side. Substitute Beuzelin claimed a consolation effort near the end but Celts were already home and dry by then.

12.3.05: Celtic 6 Dunfermline 0
Although it was only a John Hartson effort that separated the teams at the break, five goals in the second forty-five completely destroyed David Hay's Fifers who, to be fair, had serious injury problems prior to kick-off. The names on Celtic's other five goals belonged to McGeady, Hartson (his 24th in all competitions), Petrov (a double for the first time this season) and substitute Craig Beattie who nodded home right at the death to make it a super six Saturday.

16.3.05: Inverness CT 0 Celtic 2
After hitting Hibernian for three and then stealing a point at Ibrox, Craig Brewster's side naturally approached this midweek home encounter full of confidence. Craig Bellamy proved to be the real star on a bleak Inverness evening, both scoring his third goal in five games and winning the late penalty that was subsequently converted by Alan Thompson. It had been a tough tussle but, once again, Celtic proved their worth and moved yet closer to leaders Rangers in the title race. With a game in hand, O'Neill's men were now only one point behind.

19.3.05: Dundee United 2 Celtic 3
Man of the match Craig Bellamy became the first Celt to hit three in any SPL game of the season when his stunning hat-trick secured full points in the clash with Dundee United. The Welshman's first (in just five minutes) was a superb hit with the outside of his right foot from the angle of the penalty area. After McIntyre had equalised, Bellamy claimed his second shortly before the break with a finish, from Ulrik Laursen's excellent pass, which clipped woodwork on the way home. His winner (after Robson had made it 2-2 with some 20 minutes remaining) was rifled past Bullock following a long kick by Rab Douglas and flick by Sutton. Before all three points were safe, however, Douglas had to produce a wonderful save right at the end to deny Robson his second of the afternoon.

April 2005
2.4.05: Celtic 0 Hearts 2
Celtic suffered their third home defeat of the league season, leaving the title race still in the balance. After just twenty minutes, visitors Hearts were two in front (following goals from on loan striker Lee Miller and ex-Celt

Mark Burchill) and heading towards their first victory at Celtic Park since February 2000.

13.4.05: Livingston 0 Celtic 4
Having been without a goal to his name for a month, John Hartson fired Celts to the top of the league with a stunning hat-trick. His first (shortly before the interval) was a fierce left foot drive, his second a strong header and his third a penalty conversion after being fouled in the box. Stan Varga completed the rout with a stoppage time tap-in.

16.4.05: Celtic 3 Aberdeen 2
The last time Aberdeen had visited Celtic Park, they were two up with less than ten minutes on the clock. On this occasion, it took the Pittodrie outfit a few extra minutes to gain the same advantage, however, a towering header from Varga narrowed the gap before that man Hartson (from an Agathe cross early in the second period) levelled with a half-volley into the net. The winner was an absolute peach from Craig Bellamy and the crowd's reaction to his soaring volley nearly lifted the roof off the stadium.

24.4.05: Rangers 1 Celtic 2
Celtic remained on course to retain their SPL trophy after this crucial Ibrox victory. Arching his body for an Agathe cross, Stilian Petrov opened the scoring with a wonderful header before Craig Bellamy some ten minutes before the break silenced the home support with a stunning right foot drive into the bottom corner following Thompson's long ball from defence. Although Rangers pulled one back near the end of the game, there was no doubt that the visitors thoroughly deserved the three points that took them five clear at the top of the championship table.

30.4.05: Celtic 1 Hibernian 3
One week later, Celtic, minus both Bellamy and Sutton, suffered their third defeat in just six home games when Tony Mowbray's young side ran out winners at Celtic Park. Hibs had gone ahead courtesy of O'Connor in the first half and although Craig Beattie equalised with an acrobatic finish early in the second period, late goals from Brown and substitute Sproule secured the valuable points.

May 2005
8.5.05: Celtic 2 Aberdeen 0
In the last home game of the season, a John Hartson second-half double made all the headlines as Celtic regained top spot in the league table. His first of a glorious sunny Sunday afternoon, following a Thompson delivery into the penalty area, was a 'shot' that spun off his shin into the net despite Considine's determined efforts to clear off his line. Then, twenty minutes before the end, he buried from close range after Chris Sutton had fired a super low drive into the box. Interestingly, Celtic and Rangers had now swapped places at the top of the league nine times this season.

15.5.05: Hearts 1 Celtic 2
Celtic, with seven players over the age of 30 in the starting line-up, closed in on the league title with this hard fought win away to a spirited Hearts team. There was just one goal in the first period, scored by Alan Thompson who drilled past Gordon from close range after some poor defending by the home side. Although Hartley equalised in the second half, title-chasing Celts, with some thirteen minutes to go, went ahead when Craig Beattie fired emphatically beneath the keeper. It was a goal fit to win any game.

22.5.05: Motherwell 2 Celtic 1
After Chris Sutton had given his side a first half lead, Celtic created numerous opportunities to kill the game but surprisingly failed to score. Then, with the title just minutes away, Australian Scott McDonald not only equalised but also netted the winner right at the death to hand the title to Rangers who had won at Easter Road. It was an astonishing end to Celtic's SPL campaign.

Season 2004/05 – Quiz

How much can you remember about last season? Test your memory with some easy - and not so easy - questions! Answers on page 60.

1. Who scored for Celtic on the opening day of the SPL campaign?

2. How many Scots were in the starting line-up that day?

3. Prior to Christmas, only one game was credited with an official attendance of over 59,000. Who were Celtic's opponents on this occasion?

4. Who claimed the first hat-trick of the domestic campaign?

5. Where did Celtic drop their first league points last season?

6. Name the SPL opponents when defender Bobo Balde netted a rare double.

7. Can you name the four Celts who scored in Europe last season?

8. Who kept goal when Celtic recorded a wonderful 1-1 draw against Barcelona in the Nou Camp?

9. He claimed the winner in the late August Old Firm clash. Name the player.

10. How many league goals did Henri Camara score during his time at Celtic Park?

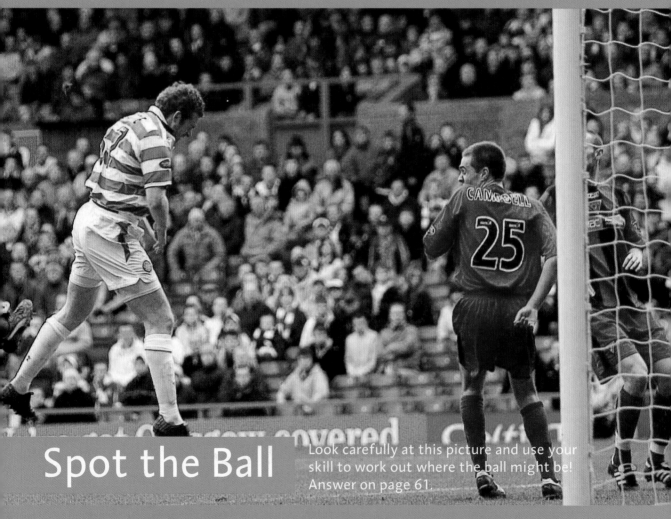

Spot the Ball

Look carefully at this picture and use your skill to work out where the ball might be!
Answer on page 61.

Spot the Difference

Study the two pictures below and try to spot the 12 differences between them (we've given you a start with the first difference). Answers on page 61.

30 Beauties
From the Big Man

Striker John Hartson ended the 2004/05 campaign at the very top of the charts with a total of 30 goals to his name. How many of them do you remember?

1 KILMARNOCK (away, 14.8.04): Following Jackie McNamara's long ball, his first of the season was a left-foot shot that went in off the post.

2 KILMARNOCK (away, 14.8.04): A header from Alan Thompson's perfect free-kick was his second of the game.

3 INVERNESS (away, 22.8.04): Another superb header but this time from a Didier Agathe cross.

4 INVERNESS (away, 22.8.04): The keeper could not hold a Valgaeren effort and Hartson buried from close range.

5 DUNDEE (home, 11.9.04): Thompson's cross, Hartson's control and then a left-foot drive some eight yards from goal.

6 HIBERNIAN (away, 19.9.04): A simple tap-in following good work by both Thompson and Brazilian Juninho.

7 HEARTS (home, 16.10.04): Ross Wallace delivered with accuracy into the box and Hartson headed past Gordon in goal.

8 LIVINGSTON (away, 24.10.04): The pace of Henri Camara created the chance for the Welshman to tap-in from six yards.

9 ABERDEEN (home, 27.10.04): Another close range conversion after being set-up by Chris Sutton.

10 ABERDEEN (home, 27.10.04): Following Stanislav Varga's cross, this strike was a ferocious volley that went in off substitute keeper Esson.

11 RANGERS (away, 10.11.04): A back post header from Thompson's inviting cross.

12 INVERNESS (home, 13.11.04): A McNamara cross, a Sutton touch and then a trademark thunderous volley that had goal written all over it.

13 INVERNESS (home, 13.11.04): McNamara was again involved and the move finished with a relatively easy nod home from just one yard.

14 BARCELONA (away, 24.11.04): His only European goal of the season was a tap-in after Varga had headed on a Stilian Petrov free-kick into the box.

15 DUNDEE (away, 28.11.04): Another tap-in finish following a mazy Aiden McGeady run past several defenders.

16 HIBERNIAN (home, 4.12.04): McGeady, from a corner, was again the supplier but this time the finish was a powerful header.

17 HIBERNIAN (home, 4.12.04): Bursting through between the centre-backs, Hartson slotted home after a delightful McGeady ball.

18 LIVINGSTON (home, 2.1.05): A header from Thompson's accurate cross.

19 RANGERS (home, 9.1.05): His second Old Firm strike of the season (and late winner) was a deflected shot off defender Andrews from a tight angle.

20 DUNFERMLINE (away, 5.2.05): On the plastic pitch, it was a simple tap-in from Sutton's low drive across goal.

21 DUNFERMLINE (away, 5.2.05): A right-foot drive from the edge of the box after Sutton's flick created the chance.

22 HIBERNIAN (away, 6.3.05): Thompson was the provider for this half-volley into the net.

23 DUNFERMLINE (home, 12.3.05): From close range, the Welshman forced home courtesy of a wicked Thompson in-swinging free-kick.

24 DUNFERMLINE (home, 12.3.05): The ball was bundled over the line after the keeper failed to hold Craig Bellamy's powerful drive into the box following a short corner.

25 LIVINGSTON (away, 13.4.05): Following McNamara's cross, his first of the evening was a fierce left-foot drive that took a deflection before beating McKenzie in goal.

26 LIVINGSTON (away, 13.4.05): A strong header, in a crowded area, from Thompson's cross into the box.

27 LIVINGSTON (away, 13.4.05): A penalty, hit perfectly with his right foot, completed the hat-trick.

28 ABERDEEN (home, 16.4.05): His well-taken strike on the half-volley brought Celtic level after they were 2-0 behind early-on in this league clash.

29 ABERDEEN (home, 8.5.05): Following Thompson's free-kick into the box, the ball spun off his shin into the net for the crucial opener in the last home game of the season.

30 ABERDEEN (home, 8.5.05): his second that day was a point-blank finish after Chris Sutton drilled a perfect low cross into the area.

Headline News

Celtic made the following football headlines during Season 2004/05. What was the occasion? The clue is in the date! Answers on page 60.

1 TOP BHOY AND THE LOST BOYS
Daily Mail, 25.4.05

2 DING-DONG BELL
Sunday Times, 17.4.05

3 SUTTON SEALS PARKHEAD STROLL
Sunday Times, 19.12.04

4 HARTSON HAULS THE BHOYS OUT OF A HOLE
Mail on Sunday, 5.12.04

5 CARELESS CELTIC LAMENT LOVELL
Daily Mail, 29.11.04

6 BEATTIE BAILS OUT CELTIC
Sunday Times, 31.10.04

7 THE PERFECT WAY TO SAY GOODBYE
Daily Mail, 30.5.05

8 HARTSON HAILED A HERO AGAIN
Daily Mail, 9.5.05

9 ALL GUNS BLAZING
Daily Mail, 22.4.05

10 CELTIC'S SIXTH SENSE
Sunday Times, 13.3.05

The Number is Celtic

Major Clue: Every answer is a number between 1 and 100!   Answers on page 60.

1. How many times have Celtic gone beyond the quarter-final stage of the European Cup?

2. If you multiply this number by ten, you will get Henrik Larsson's Celtic career goal total.

3. Before leaving the club in 1978, legendary manager Jock Stein had guided the club to how many league championships?

4. When Celtic won the Old Firm league clash of September 2001, it completed their first back-to-back Ibrox win for quite some time. How many years had it been?

5. How many goals have Celtic scored in the final of European competitions?

6. Paul McStay has been capped for Scotland more times than any other Celt in history. How many times did he wear the dark blue of his country?

7. In his first season at the club, John Hartson made 35 league and cup appearances. What was his goal total for that 2001/02 season?

8. How many goals were scored in the remarkable Old Firm League Cup Final of 1957?

9. More than one Celtic player has scored a hat-trick in the final of the League Cup competition. Do you know how many?

10. How many times was legend Billy McNeill a league championship winner?

THE EUROPEAN CUP 1967

Against all the odds, in Lisbon's Estadio Nacional, a team of all-Scottish players defeated the Italian might of Inter Milan (twice former winners) to become the first British team to lift the European Cup. Goals from Tommy Gemmell (after Inter had taken the lead) and Steve Chalmers were priceless. Along the way, the champions of Switzerland (Zurich), France (Nantes), Yugoslavia (Vojvodina) and Czechoslovakia (Dukla Prague) had all fallen by the wayside. Has there ever been a better day in the history of Scottish Football?

Celtic: Simpson, Craig, Gemmell, Murdoch, McNeill, Clark, Johnstone, Wallace, Chalmers, Auld and Lennox.

THE CORONATION CUP 1953

The top clubs of the time from both north and south of the border - Arsenal, Manchester United, Tottenham Hotspur, Newcastle, Celtic, Rangers, Hibernian and Aberdeen - took part in this extremely prestigious competition. After disposing of English Champions Arsenal 1-0, Celtic then defeated Manchester United (conquerors of Rangers) 2-1 before facing Hibernian (victors over Spurs and Newcastle) in the final. Goals from Mochan and Walsh ensured that this unique trophy would have a permanent place in the Celtic Park trophy rooms.

Celtic: Bonnar, Haughney, Rollo, Evans, Stein, McPhail, Collins, Walsh, Mochan, Peacock and Fernie.

THE GLASGOW EXHIBITION CUP 1902

A mini-tournament in support of the victims of the Ibrox disaster of 1902 comprised the champions and runners-up from England (Everton and Sunderland) as well as both Celtic and Rangers. After Celtic beat Sunderland and Rangers defeated Everton, the Old Firm contested the final which ended all-square at 1-1. The Hoops eventually took this spectacular piece of silverware home following a 3-2 extra-time victory over their great rivals. Interestingly, the actual trophy is engraved 'Won by Rangers FC' as it was originally the property of Rangers after they won the Glasgow International Tournament the previous year.

Celtic Squad: Battles, Loney, Marshall, Moir, McMahon, Watson, Campbell, Orr, McPherson, McLeod, Somers, Quinn, McMenemy, McCafferty, Crawford, McDermott, Hamilton.

THE ST MUNGO CUP 1951

As part of the Festival of Britain celebrations, this tournament involved all sixteen of the First Division clubs in Scotland. Celtic eliminated Hearts, Clyde and Raith Rovers in succession before the final confrontation with Aberdeen on the first day of August. Behind two nil in the early stages of the game (for the third time in this particular competition), Celtic eventually triumphed 3-2 with inside-forward Walsh, an every round scorer, netting the winner before an 80,000 Hampden crowd. Believe it or not, the cup itself is actually an old yachting trophy and as such is detailed with mermaids, fish and other reminders of both sea and ocean!

Celtic: Hunter, Haughney, Rollo, Evans, Mallan, Baillie, Collins, Walsh, Fallon, Peacock and Tully.

THE EMPIRE EXHIBITION TROPHY 1938

This competition was held at Ibrox (the stadium was close to Bellahouston Park where the Empire Exhibition was being staged)

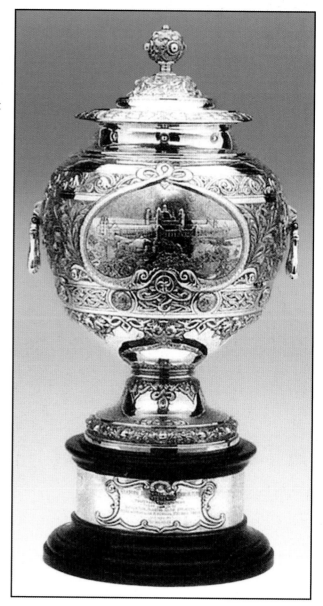

and included teams from both Scotland and England. Celtic, after wins over Sunderland (3-1) and Hearts(1-0), reached the final and faced the might of Everton (with no fewer than ten internationalists in their ranks) who had earlier disposed of Rangers. With 82,000 spectators watching, this clash of the giants went to extra-time, after a no-scoring ninety minutes, before Johnny Crum netted the only goal of the game.

Celtic: Kennaway, Hogg, Morrison, Geatons, Lyon, Paterson, Delaney, MacDonald, Crum, Divers and Murphy.

Jock Stein
– Celtic's Greatest-Ever Manager

As a player, centre-half Jock Stein was captain of the Celtic side that famously won the 1953 Coronation Cup, a tournament that comprised the best of Scotland and England at that time with Arsenal, Manchester United, Tottenham Hotspur, Newcastle, Rangers, Hibernian, Aberdeen and Celtic all taking part. In Season 1953/54, he also led Celts to their first League and Scottish Cup double for forty years. Although the above occasions were special to say the least, his greatest triumphs with Celtic were to come in a different role with the club.

Before arriving to take charge of the club in March 1965, Jock Stein ('The Big Man') had tasted managerial success at both Dunfermline and Hibernian. He transformed the Fifers into a formidable footballing outfit and famously guided them to a Scottish Cup triumph over Celtic in 1961. Then, during a short spell with Hibernian, Stein led the Easter Road side to the Summer Cup of 1964 as well as defeating Rangers in the quarter-final of the 1965 Scottish Cup competition, just days before arriving to take command at Celtic Park.

At the end of that first season (1964/65), Celtic lifted the Scottish Cup after defeating Dunfermline 3-2 at Hampden. The following 1965/66 league campaign was number one of the never to be forgotten nine-in-a-row sequence as Stein forged Celtic into a force that strode both the domestic and European stages like a colossus. His record really does speak for itself:

1964/65 – Scottish Cup.

1965/66 – League Championship, League Cup and semi-final of the European Cup Winners Cup.

1966/67 – League Championship, Scottish Cup, League Cup, Glasgow Cup and, of course, the European Cup.

1967/68 – League Championship, League Cup and Glasgow Cup.

1968/69 – League Championship, Scottish Cup, League Cup and quarter-final of the European Cup.

1969/70 – League Championship, League Cup, Glasgow Cup and the final of the European Cup.

1970/71 – League Championship, Scottish Cup and quarter-final of the European Cup.

1971/72 – League Championship, Scottish Cup and semi-final of the European Cup.

1972/73 – League Championship.

1973/74 – League Championship, Scottish Cup and semi-final of the European Cup.

1974/75 – Scottish Cup, League Cup and joint winners of the Glasgow Cup.

1975/76 – quarter-final of the European Cup Winners Cup (Sean Fallon deputised this season after Stein suffered severe injuries in a car crash.)

1976/77 – League Championship and Scottish Cup.

Somehow the word 'legend' is not quite enough when considering the Celtic career of Jock Stein.

Celtic Greats Quiz

1. Although my misplaced pass led to an opposition goal in my first game for the club, I was part of the team that lifted both the League Championship and League Cup that season. Before leaving Celtic, I created several records including a post-war one of fifteen Old Firm goals. Who am I?

   ——————— ———————

2. My nickname has Italian origins and I served the club as player, captain and manager. One of my famous goals was the last-gasp winner in the quarter-final of a rather special cup competition in the year that European glory was on the horizon. Who am I?

   ——————— ———————

3. I have been one half of high scoring football partnerships in more than one country although my skills are sometimes required at the other end of the park. At Hampden, there have been highs and lows and, on one occasion, I snapped my wrist following a penalty-box collision with a team-mate. Who am I?

   ——————— ———————

4. Did you know that I scored direct from a corner not only in a Scottish Cup tie with Falkirk but also on international duty against England? I was also a member of the great side that created a Scottish League Cup Final scoring record many years ago. Who am I?

   ———————— ——————

5. I was born in the Dalmarnock area of Glasgow and played for Possil YM as a youngster. I scored from the penalty spot on my Old Firm debut and went on to become captain of an extremely successful Celtic side before joining another club for a record British transfer fee of £440,000. Who am I?

   ——————— ———————

6. A Scot, I was something of a penalty king during my years with Celtic and netted thirty-one times from thirty-four attempts. Probably my most famous goal, however, was an equaliser away from home! Who am I?

   —————— ————————

7. During my time with Newcastle, I enjoyed FA Cup success on two separate occasions. Although hardly a youngster when I subsequently left Hibernian for Celtic (they called me 'Faither'), I was to enjoy the highlight of my playing career at the club. Who am I?

   ——————— ————————

8. Over a fifteen-year Celtic playing career, I amassed 550 goals, hitting eight of them in just one league game when the Fifers of Dunfermline were destroyed 9-0. I went on to become manager of the club some years later. Who am I?

   —————— ————————

9. In addition to Scottish League Championship success on four occasions, I won 80 caps for my country and played in the finals of both the European Championships and the World Cup. I was also assistant manager to another Celtic great when he was at Reading. Who am I?

   ———— ————————

10. When I was sixteen, I broke my neck in a car accident and was told by a specialist that I would never play football again. I have worn the colours of teams both north and south of the border. Who am I?

    —————— —————————

Answers on page 60.

A Year in theLife of Celtic

...but can you recall the actual year?

2005 1970 1988 1957 1982 1991 1974 1998 2002 1988 1973 1995 2003 1967 1966 1972 2001 1970 1977 1968 2000

1. The year that the 'unbeatable' English Champions Leeds United were defeated both home and away in the European Cup.

2. The year that Rangers were crushed 7-1 in the final of the League Cup.

3. The year that manager Billy McNeill guided the club to the 'Centenary Double' of League Championship and Scottish Cup.

4. The year that nine-in-a-row was confirmed.

5. The year that the ten-in-a-row Rangers dream was shattered.

6. The year that Henrik Larsson became the most prolific scorer for any Scottish club in Europe.

7. The year that the domestic treble was achieved by Martin O'Neill.

8. The year that saw Hibernian thrashed 6-1 in the final of the Scottish Cup.

9. The year that saw Rangers humbled 5-1 when Celtic claimed their first league title in twelve years.

10. The year that Celtic won the BBC Sportsview 'Team of the Year' trophy.

Answers on page 60.

The Players

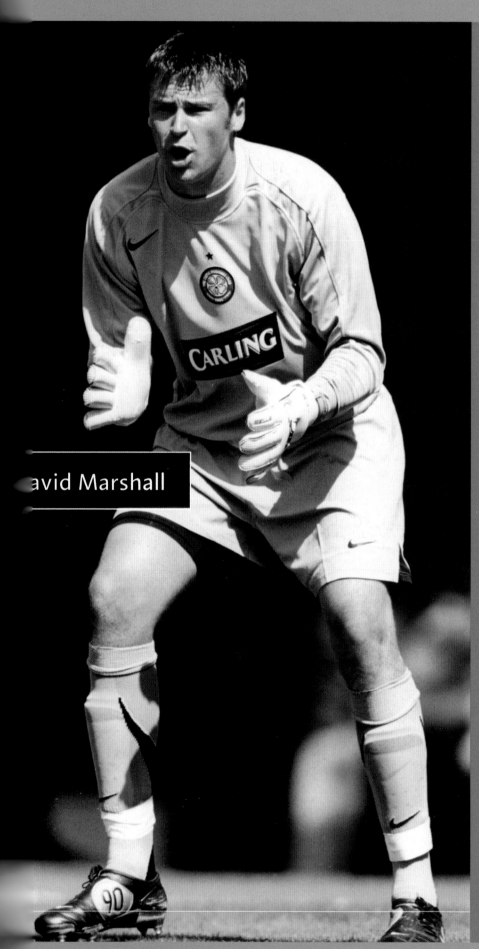

avid Marshall

The young goalkeeper, a Scotland international, was the manager's first choice for 18 out of the initial 19 domestic and European fixtures at the start of last season. Magnus Hedman (8 times) and Rab Douglas (14 times) then filled the position before Marshall was back between the posts for the 2-0 home victory over Hearts in early April. It was then a case of six consecutive appearances before Douglas returned for the remaining four 2004/05 games. Few have forgotten his wonderful teenage display at the Nou Camp Stadium in March 2004 when the strikers of Barcelona were denied time after time thus ensuring Celtic reached the quarter-final of that season's UEFA Cup tournament. Marshall signed a new four year deal shortly after this game. At Ibrox in April 2005 as the season reached a crucial stage, the young man was both confident and impressive when Celtic won 2-1 at the home of their greatest rivals. Exceptionally good at handling crosses into the box, he is a young man with a big future.

Before arriving in Glasgow, Polish goalkeeper Artur Boruc (born late February 1980) established his reputation at Legia Warszawa where he was also club captain. The 6ft 3in stopper made 26 appearances in both the 2003/04 and 2004/05 campaigns and, rather famously in his homeland, scored from the penalty spot during that former season. He actually wanted to be a striker before settling on the position of goalkeeper. At international level, the muscular Boruc has 7 caps to his name and, at present, is second-in-line behind the established Jerzy Dudek. After joining Celtic on-loan in the summer of 2005, he was given his debut by manager Gordon Strachan in the July pre-season friendly against Craig Levein's Leicester at the impressive Walkers Stadium. On that balmy summer's evening, he was called into action almost immediately and, in just the second minute of play, superbly saved a penalty from veteran Dion Dublin by diving to his left and pushing the ball past the post. He then continued to delight the huge travelling support with a confident, agile display of penalty box dominance for the rest of the ninety minutes. An impressive debut, to say the least!

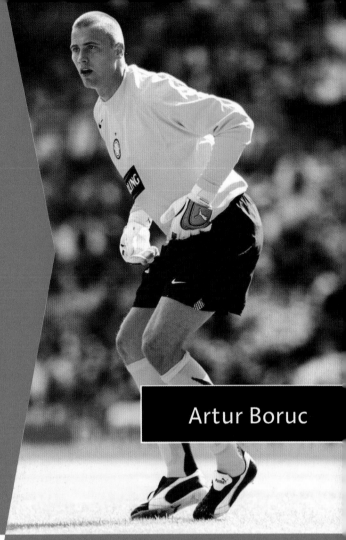

Artur Boruc

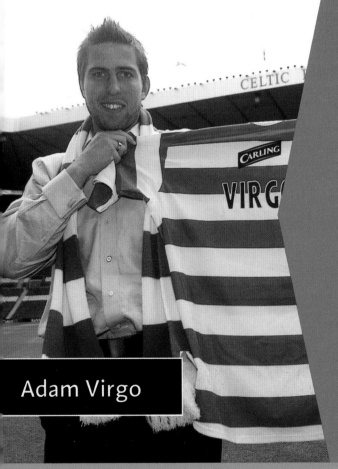

Adam Virgo

Signed from English Championship side Brighton before the start of Season 2005/06, the Scotland future defender is versatile in the extreme and actually filled a variety of roles in Mark McGhee's Sussex side. At various times, the 22-year-old Virgo was centre-half, right full-back, striker and, most impressively against Tottenham Hotspur in the FA Cup, the left-sided man in a back three formation. On the final day of last season in the crucial clash with Ipswich, it was his name on the goal that enabled Brighton to escape relegation and remain in the Championship. Not surprisingly, he lifted the Seagulls' Player of the Year award for that campaign. A fine athlete with a superb attitude, Virgo is an exceptional young talent.

Mo Camara

Four days before his 30th birthday, in late June 2005, Guinean defender Mo Camara became Gordon Strachan's first Celtic signing. The speedy, experienced left-back had an excellent 2004/05 season with Burnley in England and was watched by club scout Tom O'Neill over a period of time before putting pen to paper on a two-year Celtic deal. Despite interest from Craig Levein's Leicester, the Bosman signing had no doubts about coming to Glasgow and said at the time: 'This really is a dream come true for me – I didn't think one day I would end up playing for a massive club like Celtic. They really do seem to have the best fans in the world. Everywhere I've been I've met them – in America, in the Dominican Republic and all over Britain.' African Camara, who forged a close friendship with Alex Rae of Rangers during their time together at Wolves, is the type of honest, hard working player whose commitment to the jersey is second to none.

Although the young Scottish striker did not actually start any games last season, his 13 substitute appearances resulted in a total of four goals for the team. In addition to his strikes in the home clashes against Dunfermline (6-0, 12.3.05) and Hibernian (1-3, 30.4.05), Beattie also claimed the crucial winners at Fir Park against Motherwell (3-2, 30.10.04) and at Tynecastle when Hearts were beaten 2-1 in the penultimate league game of the 2004/05 campaign. Early-on in Season 2005/06, the hit man was continuing to impress and netted in the opening two SPL championship games at Fir Park and Celtic Park respectively. In their own way, both goals were of the 'rather special' variety. Firstly, against Motherwell on the opening day of the league season, his injury time strike earned the side a share of the spoils when it really looked as if the points were lost (4-4, 30.7.05) and, secondly, in the following week's 2-0 win over Dundee United, his thunderous first-time volley (from an excellent Shaun Maloney cross into the box) was a supreme example of the goalscoring art. There is no doubt that Craig Beattie will be pushing hard for a place in Gordon Strachan's starting eleven.

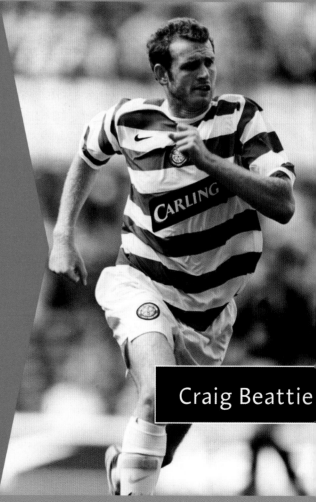

Craig Beattie

Last season, the Slovak defender's 34 SPL outings followed-on from his 35 league appearances from the previous 2003/04 period. Varga, who enjoyed a truly exceptional campaign for the club, hit six goals both home and abroad as Celtic battled on all fronts. Although his first two strikes came in consecutive outings, the actual games were as similar as chalk and cheese. His opener in the September stroll with Dunfermline at Celtic Park (3-0) was followed four days later with a magnificent headed equaliser against AC Milan in the San Siro that would have earned O'Neill's side a first away point in the Champions League tournament but for two cruel Italian blows late-on. Regarding Europe, it is also worth noting that his head-on from a Petrov free-kick supplied John Hartson for the equaliser against Barcelona in the Nou Camp in November's superb Celtic display. The following February, Varga hit a double in the Scottish Cup tie with Clyde at Broadwood (a header and tap-in from close range were two fifths of a total of 5) before netting in consecutive outings again when Livingston and Aberdeen provided the April SPL opposition, away and home respectively. Considering his towering performance in the Old Firm victory at Ibrox in April, it is not hard to come to the conclusion that there are few better defenders in the Scottish game at present.

Stanislav Varga

Didier Agathe

Mainly because of injury, Didier Agathe only started 22 games in the 2004/05 period. In January 2005, after some weeks on the sidelines for that very reason, he returned for the crucial Scottish Cup tie with Rangers at Celtic Park. After this win on the road to Hampden, manager Martin O'Neill commented: 'I have never known a player who could come back like that. It was one of his best Old Firm games. Didier was outstanding. He took it upon himself to not only do a superb defensive job but he was also wonderful going forward.' Unfortunately, subsequent Achilles and groin problems meant that the player required surgery and he was then missing from the starting line-up until – wait for it – the next Old Firm clash which was at Ibrox in late April. Once again, Agathe was quite excellent with a solid performance and, additionally, he was supplier of the cross for Celtic's first goal (courtesy of Stilian Petrov) in the 2-1 SPL victory. Nobody would dispute the fact that, for £35,000, he has been a fantastic buy for the club.

It comes as little surprise to note that no other Celtic player made more starting appearances last season than Neil Lennon whose total for the 2004/05 period was 49 European and domestic outings including a complete SPL campaign. Regularly chastised by opposition fans the length and breadth of the country, the midfielder (a quite superb reader of the game) rarely has a bad ninety minutes and, for the five seasons when Martin O'Neill was in charge of the club, was the manager's trusted on-field lieutenant. In many ways, during that hugely successful time, it was impossible to imagine a Celtic side taking to the field without the fiery, resolute redhead. During the 2004/05 period, the manager's comment that 'he carries as many injuries and illnesses as any player who plays half the games that he plays' really summed-up the wee man's attitude to playing for Celtic. Although it has been said before on numerous occasions, it is certainly worth repeating the obvious - the Irishman's value to the team just cannot be underestimated. Gordon Strachan appointed him team captain for Season 2005/06.

Neil Lennon

Stilian Petrov

Surely the best goalscoring midfielder in the SPL at present, Stilian Petrov (both Celtic Player of the Year and Celtic Players' Player of the Year for Season 2004/05) enjoyed another marvellous campaign last time round and was one of only three players - the others being John Hartson and Neil Lennon – to achieve 49 starts for the club. Also third top scorer with 12 goals, the Bulgarian's pre-Christmas total of four was doubled to eight more in the period from Boxing Day until the end of May. During that latter period, he netted in four consecutive outings when Clyde (5-0, 27.2.05), Dundee (3-0, 2.3.05), Hibernian (3-1, 6.3.05) and Dunfermline (6-0, 12.3.05) were all put to the sword. Indeed, he claimed a double in the 6-0 drubbing of Dunfermline at Celtic Park. Two of his best strikes last season were away from home, at East End Park and Ibrox. His wonderful scissor-kick volley against Dunfermline (see '5 Goals of the Season' article in the annual) was more than complemented by his stunning header against Rangers in the April Old Firm joust that Celtic clinched 2-1.

Blessed with superb vision and a brilliant touch, the Japanese creative midfielder joined Celtic after spending three years in Italy with Reggina (where he scored in his very first outing against Taranto in August 2002), having played a total of 80 Serie A games with the European club. Such was his impact in Italy that Reggina released a statement at the time of his transfer to Celtic that included the following paragraph: 'The club feels it is necessary to express the affection and appreciation for the great human, technical and professional qualities - as well as the strong attachment to the jersey - he has shown in the last three years.' Born in Yokohama in June 1978, he was a standout performer for his country in both the 2004 Asian Cup and the 2005 Confederations Cup with his display against Brazil in the latter tournament particularly impressive. Indeed, alongside Hideo Nakata, he is the most famous footballer in Japan and a true icon in that part of the world. Prior to his arrival in Glasgow, manager Gordon Strachan was quoted as saying: 'He has good vision going forward and can see a pass, which a lot of people can't see. He is also brave on the ball and is a decent lad, too. He was a star against Brazil in the Confederations Cup, scored a goal and won the Man-of-the-match award. Not just any player can do that.'

Shunsuke Nakamura

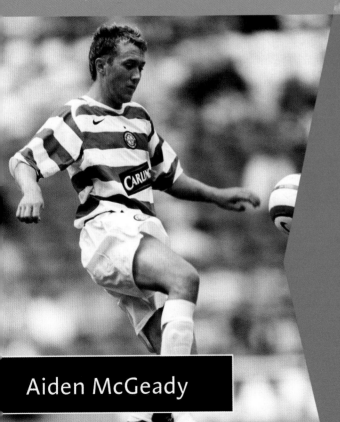

Aiden McGeady

A rare talent, the sure-footed youngster — such a joy to watch on any football park - began 25 games throughout Season 2004/05 and hit five goals in the jousts with Falkirk (8-1, 21.9.04), Motherwell (3-2, 30.10.04), Kilmarnock (2-1, 6.11.04), Hearts (2-0, 26.12.04) and Dunfermline (6-0, 12.3.05). One of his most memorable displays of the campaign was on European duty at Celtic Park in December. Few Celtic fans have forgotten McGeady's mesmerising performance in this Champions League clash with AC Milan in Glasgow when he tormented (with a capital T!) right full-back Fabricio Coloccini. After the game, the legendary Paolo Maldini said: 'He has talent, a good personality and calmness. Celtic lack a player who can beat people, who can do something different to alter the course of a game and perhaps he can become it.' The following February, at just 18-years-of-age, the Celt earned his third international cap for the Republic of Ireland in the clash with Portugal at Lansdowne Road in Dublin when Brian Kerr's side extended their unbeaten run to eight games. Not surprisingly, McGeady was voted Young Player of the Year at the Celtic Player of the Year awards in May 2005.

Alan Thompson

Scoring in both the first and final games away from Celtic Park last season (Kilmarnock in the SPL and Dundee United in the Scottish Cup Final), the midfielder's uncannily accurate left-foot crosses (or corners) into the box, once again, provided the creative platform for others to supply the finishing touch. However, it was the Englishman who, understandably, lifted the Goal of the Season award at the Celtic Player of the Year event for his sublime strike in the first Old Firm clash of the 2004/05 period - the second time in two years that Thompson had been honoured this way. Not bad for a midfielder! Thompson, under contract until the summer of 2007, actually netted a total of 10 in his 43 starts for Celtic last season with four strikes in consecutive outings – Motherwell (3-2, 30.10.04), Shakhtar Don (1-0, 2.11.04), Kilmarnock (2-1, 6.11.04) and Rangers (1-2, 10.11.04). Indeed, his goal in the Champions League tie with Shakhtar Don ensured a first Group F win for Celtic after four European outings. Right at the end of the campaign, his strike on Scottish Cup Final day at Hampden ensured silverware was returning to the trophy rooms.

The striker (or defender!) enjoyed another marvellous campaign in Celtic's colours and ended the 2004/05 journey having made 33 starting appearances with 16 goals to his name. After scoring in the opening SPL game of the season (the 2-0 home defeat of Motherwell), his richest vein of striking came in the period from mid-December through to early February when he netted in eight out of nine consecutive fixtures. The team's beaten opponents during that period were: Dunfermline (2-0, 12.12.04), Dundee United (1-0, 18.12.04), Livingston (2-1, 2.1.05), Rangers (2-1, 9.1.05), Aberdeen (1-0, 16.1.05), Motherwell (2-0, 22.1.05), Kilmarnock (1-0, 30.1.05) and Dunfermline (3-0, 5.2.05). Sutton's goal in the aforementioned Scottish Cup tie with Rangers was his seventh in Old Firm clashes. Hampered by injury problems during the latter part of the league race, it was Sutton who scored at Fir Park on the day when the SPL title really should have been retained. Now in season number six at the club, the player – just like fellow Englishman Alan Thompson – is a Celt until the summer of 2007.

Chris Sutton

John Hartson

Scottish Football Writers' Player of the Year and joint winner of the SPFA Player of the Year award, the Welsh dragon obviously had an astonishing season. As well as being the country's top scorer with 30 competition goals (only one of which was a penalty), injury-free Hartson was one of just two players to complete the 2004/05 league campaign without missing a game. In addition to his hat-trick against Livingston in April, the striker claimed doubles on eight separate occasions - in the meetings with Kilmarnock, Inverness Caley Thistle (twice), Aberdeen (twice), Hibernian and Dunfermline (twice). His year's journey was full of obvious highlights and included a rather special night in Spain when his goal in the Nou Camp Champions League tie with Barcelona earned Celtic a share of the points, a feat not achieved by either AC Milan or Real Madrid in games at the same stadium weeks earlier. Two months later, shortly after signing a new deal that will keep him at the club until 2007 at least, big man Hartson claimed the Old Firm winner at Celtic Park when Rangers' Scottish Cup run came to an abrupt 2-1 end in the east end of the city.

After having established a formidable goalscoring record at club level in his homeland, Polish international striker Maciej Zurawski arrived at Celtic Park for the start of Season 2005/06. During that extremely prolific period with current champions Wisla Krakow, he scored over 100 championship goals and hit a rich vein of form during the latter stages of 2004/05 when he netted 24 times in 25 league games. Additionally, on the European stage, the striker claimed goals in clashes with high calibre opposition such as Parma, Schalke 04 and Lazio. After making his international debut against Slovakia back in November 1998, more recently the hitman found the back of the net against Wales (away), England (home) and Northern Ireland (away) in the 2004/05 World Cup qualifying campaign. In April 2005, fellow countryman Dariusz Wdowczyk brought the striker to the attention of the club when he was completing a UEFA coaching badge at Celtic Park. Skilful and very quick, Zurawski decided to further his career in Glasgow – despite strong interest from Trabzonspor in Turkey – and manager Gordon Strachan made him his second Celtic signing (after Mo Camara) in the summer of 2005.

Maciej Zurawsk

RANGERS 1 CELTIC 2 (Petrov, Bellamy)

Prior to kick-off, as the atmosphere built for this Old Firm clash of the titans in Govan, a banner with the words 'WELCOME TO THE CRAIG BELLAMY SHOW' was unfurled by some visiting Celtic fans. Two hours later, by the end of the game, it was apparent to both sides of the great divide that although not entirely running the show, the Welshman was certainly a star turn on the bill!

Before this encounter, Celtic were just two points ahead of Rangers at the top of the table and realised that defeat at the hands of their oldest rivals, with just four league games remaining to play, was just not an option this late on in the season. With both sides having dropped points earlier in the month, this clash had all the makings of a classic 'winner takes all' encounter.

Both sides started well and created chances but the breakthrough came for Celtic after some twenty minutes of play. With his marker Vignal failing to close him down, Didier Agathe delivered an inviting ball into the box that was attacked by both Stilian Petrov and Andrews. The Bulgarian managed to move in front of the big defender and, arching his body, produced a quite wonderful header that found the corner of the net. In the heat of the moment, he seemed to lose his bearings and his subsequent run to the Rangers fans earned a yellow card from referee Dougal.

Ten minutes later, Craig Bellamy doubled the visitors' advantage with one of the most stunning strikes seen in a long time. It all began with Alan Thompson's accurate long ball out of defence which found the running Bellamy on left wing patrol. However, with Greek defender Kyrgiakos close to hand, the hitman still had it all to do. He duly took on the big man and cut inside before releasing a deadly right-foot strike that buried itself in the bottom corner for a genuine goal of the season contender. Although Andrews hit the bar with a header late in the first period, there were no more goals before the half-time break.

Virtually right at the start of the second forty-five, Craig Bellamy left the field (to a hero's ovation from one end of the ground) after pulling up injured and, with Celtic's talisman now gone, Rangers came back into the game and David Marshall was called into action on more than one occasion. After creating several chances, the home side eventually scored via substitute Thompson shortly before the final whistle but it was a case of too little, too late and the better team ran out worthy winners on the day. There really was not a failure for Celtic with both Balde (in defence) and Sutton (in midfield) barely putting a foot wrong.

There would be more twists and turns to come in the 2004/05 championship race before the destination of the trophy was finally decided but, for today at least, all Celtic fans could enjoy the rest of a rather super sunny Sunday.

Celtic: Marshall, Agathe, Balde, Varga, McNamara, Thompson, Lennon, Sutton, Petrov, Hartson and Bellamy.

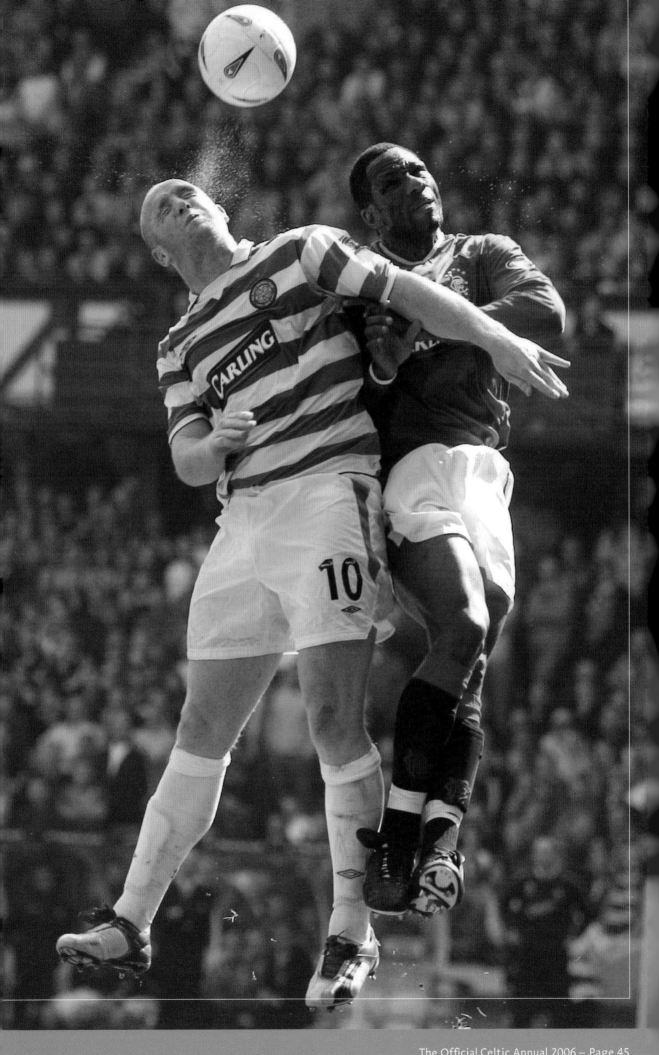

Celtic's 2005
Scottish Cup Journey

Celtic ✣

Beginning with a home game against Rangers in January, Celtic's 2005 Scottish Cup journey then took them to East End Park (to face Dunfermline), Broadwood (First Division Clyde), Hampden (Hearts in the semi-final) and, of course, Hampden again for the May final of the competition when Dundee United provided the early summer opposition.

Although Rangers won the two previous Old Firm clashes at Ibrox (the November SPL and CIS Cup games), it had been almost five long years since they last tasted victory at Celtic Park and were obviously out to make amends after being drawn away to Celtic in the competition. With both teams totally committed right from the start (referee Dallas had to deal with nearly 10 fouls in the first ten minutes), this showdown between the

two Scottish heavyweights was certainly an enthralling clash.

Some ten minutes before half-time, Celtic took the lead - and it all began with a long Douglas kick-out. John Hartson and Khizanishvili both rose to meet the descending ball with the Welshman winning a header on to Chris Sutton who broke beyond defender Andrews to net past Klos in goal. After Ricksen had equalised for the visitors (a headed goal just after the restart), Celtic turned up the heat with Petrov, McGeady and then Sutton all coming close to turning the game in their side's favour.

Another goal certainly seemed on the cards and, with barely fifteen minutes left to play, the ace in the pack proved to be that man

Hartson. Following Didier Agathe's cross from the right, the big man clipped past Klos (with the aid of a deflection off Andrews) from a tight angle in the six yard box. Although Rangers created a couple of late chances, Celtic were safely over the first hurdle in their defence of the trophy that they have won more times than any other club.

Celtic: Douglas, Agathe, Balde, Varga, Laursen, McGeady, McNamara, Thompson, Petrov, Hartson and Sutton.

At the beginning of February, Dunfermline and the artificial pitch of East End Park was the first away port of call on the Scottish Cup trail. With new signing Craig Bellamy watching from the sidelines, the game was effectively over with barely ten minutes on the clock as Martin O'Neill's men were already two to the good by that early stage of the proceedings. John Hartson (with his 20th goal of the season) opened the scoring in eight minutes when he had a simple close finish from Chris Sutton's low ball drilled into the area.

The twins of menace reversed roles just 120 seconds later with Hartson this time the provider – his volley into the box struck woodwork allowing Sutton then to head home for number two. The Hartson/Sutton combination had now hit 35 goals in Season 2004/05. The Cup holders then made it three and easy just before the half-time break when Hartson struck again with a powerful right-foot drive from Sutton's flick after a Laursen ball into the penalty area. Although there was no further scoring, Hartson did pick up a yellow card late in the game meaning that he was now automatically banned for the quarter-final encounter later in the month.

Celtic: Douglas, Henchoz, Balde, Varga, Laursen, Petrov, Lennon, Thompson, McGeady, Hartson and Sutton.

There is no doubt that, for much of the first-half of the next round game, Clyde matched Celtic stride for stride at Broadwood. However, when Stanislav Varga powered a header past Halliwell (from Juninho's corner

in forty minutes), the writing was on the wall for the First Division outfit. Right at the start of the second period, Shaun Maloney (on for Chris Sutton) was fouled in the box by Arbuckle, his former Celtic youth team-mate, with Alan Thompson converting the resultant spot-kick. Three minutes after Stilian Petrov hit the crossbar, the Bulgarian then made it three with powerful drive into the bottom corner. That was not the end of the scoring, however, and Varga claimed his second of the day with a tap-in from Thompson's corner before Craig Bellamy hit his first Celtic goal with a lovely curling shot away from the keeper. Home and dry with five!

Celtic: Douglas, Henchoz, Balde, Varga, McNamara, Petrov, Juninho, Lennon, Thompson, Bellamy and Sutton.

The week before the semi-final meeting with Hearts at Hampden, John Robertson's Tynecastle men had won at Celtic Park in the league (for the first time since February 2000) and were naturally confident of a similar outcome in the days leading up to this game. Within three minutes, however, that task had become a little less likely when Chris Sutton opened the scoring from a corner. Alan Thompson's impeccable delivery was certainly inviting and Sutton nodded home after Gordon, off his line, misjudged the flight of the ball. Shortly after the start of the second forty-five, Celtic doubled their tally after Hartson's head-flick (from Varga's free-kick) fell to Craig Bellamy who fired past Gordon. Although the Hearts keeper seemed to have it covered, the ball ended up in the back of the net for Bellamy's seventh in nine games. Hearts pulled one back via substitute Cesnauskis with thirty minutes to go but there were no additional scares after that, leaving Celtic still with the possibility of back-to-back league and cup doubles for the first time in over 30 years.

Celtic: Marshall, McNamara, Balde, Varga, Valgaeren, Petrov, Lennon, Sutton, Thompson, Bellamy and Hartson.

The week after Celtic lost their league crown and Dundee United narrowly avoided relegation from the SPL, O'Neill's men faced the Tannadice outfit (semi-final conquerors of Hibernian) in the final of the 2005 Scottish Cup at Hampden. Celtic took the lead early-on with a low Alan Thompson free-kick that was helped on its way with a United deflection past Bullock in goal. With Craig Bellamy in man-of-the-match mood, the Scottish Cup holders created several other chances but failed to capitalise. Chris Sutton even managed to miss a penalty in the second period (he slipped just as he was about to strike the ball) after Bellamy had been brought down in the box by defender Kenneth, the very same player who deflected for Celtic's solitary goal. That was the first time that any Celtic player had missed a penalty in the final of the Scottish Cup. Although Archibald hit the bar with a thunderous drive right at the end, Celtic were more than worthy winners on the day that Martin O'Neill brought down the curtain after five fabulous years in Glasgow.

Celtic: Douglas, Agathe, Balde, Varga, McNamara, Petrov, Lennon, Sutton, Thompson, Hartson and Bellamy.

5 Great Goals
of the Season

August 2004 – Alan Thompson v Rangers

With honours even and the first Old Firm clash of the season looking as if it would end with neither side taking all three points, Alan Thompson stepped forward to produce a bit of real magic late-on and unleashed an astonishing left-foot shot which swerved and dipped before finding the back of the net off the bar. Although this was only the fourth league game, the Celtic fans doubted that they would see a better strike all season.

December 2004 – Stilian Petrov v Dunfermline

For his first goal in several weeks, the Bulgarian midfielder hit a real beauty that had class, in capital letters, written all over it. Celtic, already one-up on the artificial surface, stretched their lead when the acrobatic Petrov twisted and turned in mid-air before delivering a right-foot scissor-kick volley that shot past the bemused Stillie heading for the top corner of the net.

April 2005 – Craig Bellamy v Aberdeen

Craig's cracker came early in the second period after Celtic had fought back from 2-0 behind to level the score. Direct from Alan Thompson's corner, the Welshman buried behind Esson with a truly spectacular volley that whistled in the wind before finding a resting place. And how the home crowd loved it!

April 2005 – Craig Bellamy v Rangers

Certainly, the striker still had it all to do when he picked up an Alan Thompson long ball out of defence and, with defender Kyrgiakos in close attendance, a goal did not look forthcoming. However, after cutting inside the Greek international, Bellamy hit the most accurate drive into the bottom corner to silence three sections of Ibrox stadium.

May 2005 – Alan Thompson v Dundee United

Although not as spectacular, this Alan Thompson Scottish Cup final free-kick, which in truth took a defection into the net, is just as, if not more, important than any of the above. Quite simply, it meant that not only the Scottish Cup was staying at Celtic Park for another year but also that Martin O'Neill's final season ended with silverware.

The Strachan Quiz

How much do you know about manager Gordon Strachan? Check out the following questions about his career as both player and manager BC – Before Celtic!

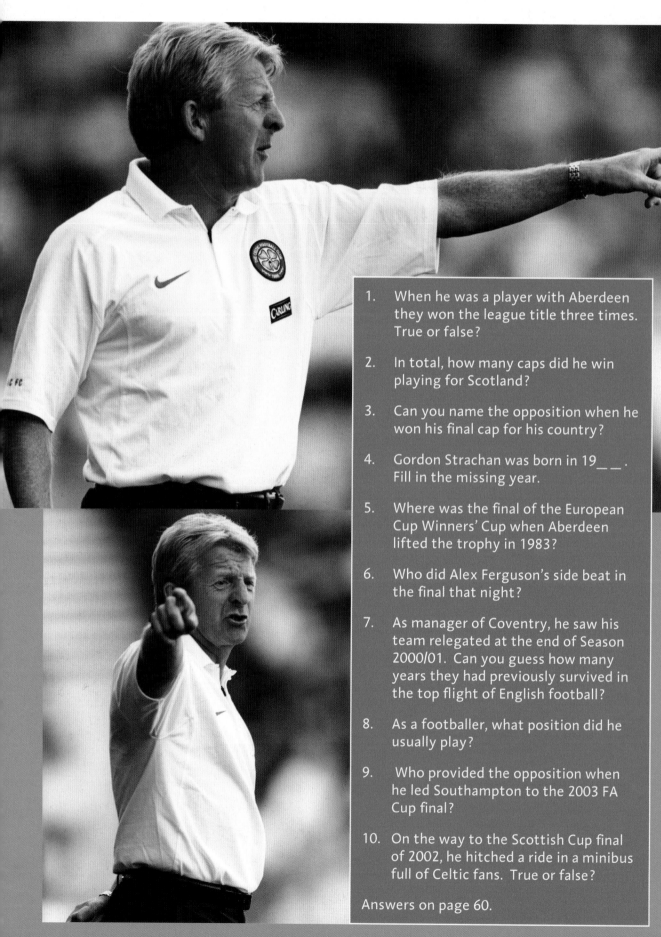

1. When he was a player with Aberdeen they won the league title three times. True or false?

2. In total, how many caps did he win playing for Scotland?

3. Can you name the opposition when he won his final cap for his country?

4. Gordon Strachan was born in 19＿＿. Fill in the missing year.

5. Where was the final of the European Cup Winners' Cup when Aberdeen lifted the trophy in 1983?

6. Who did Alex Ferguson's side beat in the final that night?

7. As manager of Coventry, he saw his team relegated at the end of Season 2000/01. Can you guess how many years they had previously survived in the top flight of English football?

8. As a footballer, what position did he usually play?

9. Who provided the opposition when he led Southampton to the 2003 FA Cup final?

10. On the way to the Scottish Cup final of 2002, he hitched a ride in a minibus full of Celtic fans. True or false?

Answers on page 60.

Celtic World Huddle

Launched in 2002, the Celtic World Huddle is the club's global membership scheme that unites Celtic supporters the world over under the banner of the beloved huddle.

The Celtic players' pre-match huddle has become an iconic image for supporters since its introduction in 1995 when player Tony Mowbray suggested the idea as a way to display team unity. The first Celtic huddle took place on 21st July before a pre-season game against German amateur side VfB Lubeck and is now a regular pre-match way for the Bhoys to display solidarity and, as such, is the perfect symbol of the global membership scheme.

The Celtic World Huddle offers various membership tiers to ensure that supporters get exactly what they are looking for from the club. Having an adult membership is the only way supporters can gain entry to the season ticket waiting list for their ticket to Paradise. For Season 2005/06, adult members also receive a free Celtic DVD, scarf, personal Celtic radio with headphones and regular membership newsletters.

Having a junior membership is the only way to be in with a chance of being selected as an official club mascot or ball bhoy/girl for most games at Celtic Park. Season 2004/05 saw lucky Celtic World Huddle members selected as home and away team mascots for all of the UEFA Champions League matches at Celtic Park where they led out the teams and experienced the amazing on-pitch atmosphere beside some of the finest players in the world!

Younger hoops fans can choose between two levels of membership suited to their age: 0-5 years and 6-16 years. This year, members in the 0-5 years group receive a great gift pack containing a personalised membership card, an inflatable swimming set including Hoopy armbands, ring and beach ball, three junior membership letters throughout the year and even special Christmas and birthday cards from the club! Members in the 6-16

years group also receive their Christmas and birthday cards and personalised membership card as well as a Celtic DVD, Celtic scarf, Celtic baseball cap, Celtic sticker set and three membership newsletters.

It could not be easier to join the Celtic World Huddle. You can: log on to www.celticfc.net and join through the online ticket office, fill out an application form at the Celtic Ticket Office or call 0870 060 1888 (for UK, Republic of Ireland and European memberships) or +44 1782 741 959 for memberships for the rest of the world.

World of Celtic

Neil
Lennon
(N. Ireland)

John
Hartson
(Wales)

David
Marshall
(Scotland)

Craig
Beattie
(Scotland)

Artur
Boruc
(Poland)

Maciej
Zurawski
(Poland)

Mo
Camara
(Guinea)

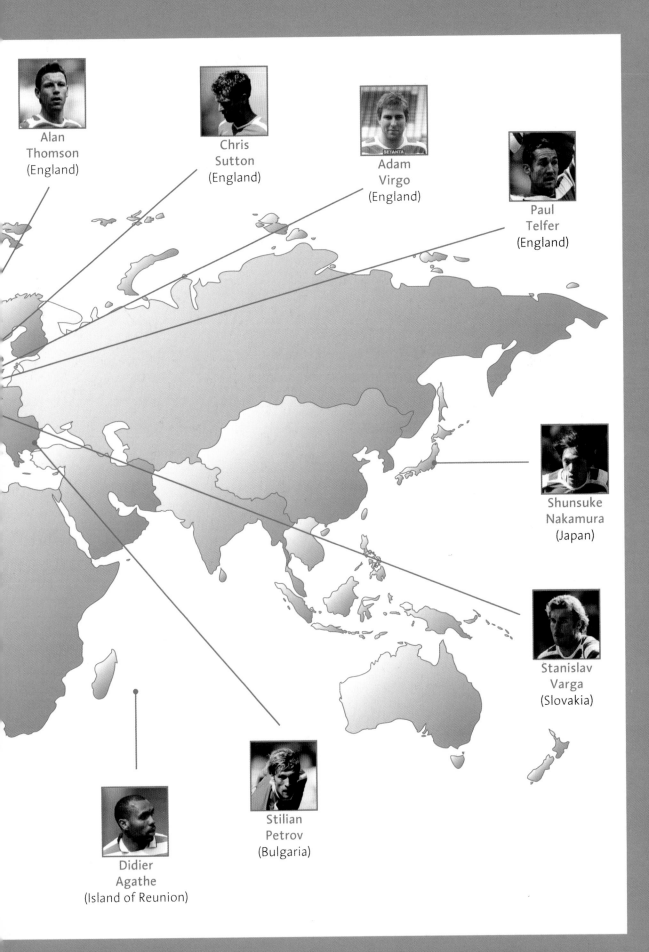

Alan
Thomson
(England)

Chris
Sutton
(England)

Adam
Virgo
(England)

Paul
Telfer
(England)

Shunsuke
Nakamura
(Japan)

Stanislav
Varga
(Slovakia)

Stilian
Petrov
(Bulgaria)

Didier
Agathe
(Island of Reunion)

The Name Game

Page 58 – The Official Celtic Annual 2006

Re-arrange the following letters to reveal the names of people, places and events associated with Celtic:

1. Quite simply, a legend - COST K NEIJ

    ____ _____

2. Only the best need apply - PUNTO PUREE HEAC

    ___ _____ ___

3. A home from home - DRAN PAH KEMP

    _____ ____

4. Gone but not forgotten - KARL IS NON SHER

    _____ _____

5. One of the true greats - LINT NOE LIMAR

    _____ _____

6. Maybe again this season - HISTONAC STOMP HICS

    _____ _____

7. Lionheart - LOVERSTAIN PIT

    _____ _____

8. It can happen again - AIN IN WOREN

    ____ __ _ ___

9. A hero in his homeland - US MAKE U RUNS A HANK

    _____ _____

10. New for 2005/06 - ROAR CUBTUR

    _____ _____

11. Before every game - DU DELTE HH

    ___ _____

12. A blast from the past - YORRG YIMM JCM

    _____ _____

13. Weaver of magic - TENN YOOS HIM JMJ

    _____ _____

14. Green and white as far as the eye could see - VILE LES

    _____

15. Both red and green - SNO TARJ HONH

    ____ _____

16. Too famous for words - NO BLIS NO SLIT EH

    ___ _____ ____

17. Home of the brave - RALE KIC TCP

    _____ ____

18. If you know the history - THE LAIRRD FORWB

    _____ _____

19. The mighty atom - YES TAPRAG HALLC

    _____ _____

20. Season 1987/88 and the - RANT LEEDY BEN COU

    _____ _____

Answers on page 60.

The Honours

Scottish League Championships (39 in total)

1892/93, 1893/94, 1895/96, 1897/98, 1904/05, 1905/06, 1906/07, 1907/08, 1908/09, 1909/10, 1913/14, 1914/15, 1915/16, 1916/17, 1918/19, 1921/22, 1925/26, 1935/36, 1937/38, 1953/54, 1965/66, 1966/67, 1967/68, 1968/69, 1969/70, 1970/71, 1971/72, 1972/73, 1973/74, 1976/77, 1978/79, 1980/81, 1981/82, 1985/86, 1987/88, 1997/98, 2000/01, 2001/02, 2003/04.

Scottish Cups (33)

1892, 1899, 1900, 1904, 1907, 1908, 1911, 1912, 1914, 1923, 1925, 1927, 1931, 1933, 1937, 1951, 1954, 1965, 1967, 1969, 1971, 1972, 1974, 1975, 1977, 1980, 1985, 1988, 1989, 1995, 2001, 2004, 2005

Scottish League Cups (12)

1956, 1957, 1965, 1966, 1967, 1968, 1969, 1974, 1982, 1997, 2000, 2001.

European Cup

Winners 1967
Runners up 1970

Uefa Cup Runners up 2003

Coronation Cup 1953

St. Mungo Cup 1951

Victory in Europe Cup 1945

Empire Exhibition Trophy 1938

Scottish League Commemorative Shield 1904/05 – 1909/10

Glasgow Exhibition Cup 1902

Quiz Answers

How much do you know about manager Gordon Strachan? Check out the following questions about his career as both player and manager BC – Before Celtic!

SEASON 2004/05 QUIZ – ANSWERS

1. Jackie McNamara and Chris Sutton.

2. Three – David Marshall, Jackie McNamara and Aiden McGeady.

3. AC Milan.

4. Ross Wallace in the CIS Cup clash with Falkirk.

5. Easter Road in the 2-2 September draw.

6. Dundee - 3-0, 2.3.05.

7. John Hartson, Stanislav Varga, Alan Thompson and Chris Sutton.

8. Magnus Hedman.

9. Alan Thompson.

10. Eight.

HEADLINE NEWS – ANSWERS

1. A fine display of goalkeeping by David Marshall in the 2-1 Ibrox victory.

2. Craig Bellamy's wonderful winner in the 3-2 game with Aberdeen.

3. Dundee United are outplayed for ninety minutes but only a Chris Sutton goal separates the sides.

4. John Hartson's late goal in the 2-1 Celtic Park win over Hibernian.

5. Steve Lovell scores twice in the 2-2 Dens Park draw with Dundee.

6. Craig Beattie scores the late winner at Fir Park in the 3-2 Motherwell win.

7. Celtic lift the Scottish Cup and Martin O'Neill says goodbye.

8. A Hartson double in the last home league game of the season.

9. Craig Bellamy promises to give his all prior to the last Old Firm clash of the campaign.

10. Celtic crush Dunfermline 6-0 in a league game.

THE NUMBER IS CELTIC – ANSWERS

1. 4 (2 finals and 2 semi-finals)
2. 24
3. 10
4. 18
5. 5
6. 76
7. 24
8. 8 (7 for Celtic and 1 for Rangers)
9. 4 (McPhail, Lennox, Deans and Larsson)
10. 13 (9 as a player and 4 as a manager)

CELTIC GREATS QUIZ – ANSWERS

1. Henrik Larrson
2. Billy McNeill
3. Chris Sutton
4. Charlie Tully
5. Kenny Dalglish
6. Tommy Gemmell
7. Ronnie Simpson
8. Jimmy McGrory
9. Pat Bonner
10. Alan Thompson

A YEAR IN THE LIFE OF CELTIC – ANSWERS

1. 1970
2. 1957
3. 1988
4. 1974
5. 1998
6. 2002
7. 2001
8. 1972
9. 1966
10. 1967

THE STRACHAN QUIZ – ANSWERS

1. False – it was twice.
2. 50.
3. Finland in 1992.
4. 57.
5. Gothenburg, Sweden.
6. Real Madrid.
7. 34 years.
8. Right-sided midfielder.
9. Arsenal
10. True!

THE NAME GAME – ANSWERS

1. Jock Stein
2. The European Cup
3. Hampden Park
4. Henrik Larsson
5. Martin O'Neill
6. Scottish Champions
7. Stilian Petrov
8. Nine in a Row
9. Shunsuke Nakamura
10. Artur Boruc
11. The Huddle
12. Jimmy Mcgrory
13. Jimmy Johnstone
14. Seville
15. John Hartson
16. The Lisbon Lions
17. Celtic Park
18. Brother Walfrid
19. Patsy Gallacher
20. Centenary Double

Did you spot the ball?

Did you spot the twelve differences?

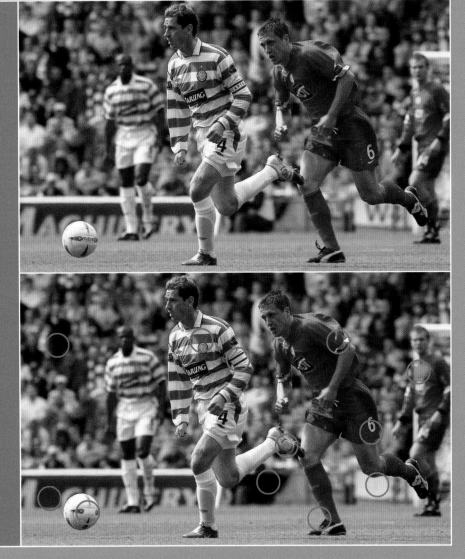